little bit of ~~something~~
so I hope ~~you~~ it can
help you to see clearly
a little ~~few~~ of the beauty
the world wants to
show.

Reading a book is
the only way a person
can be free.
Thankyou for
evrything

Juliana

God Bless you!

Discovery and Other Poems

Roberta Tinkham

VANTAGE PRESS
New York

FIRST EDITION

Copyright © 1995 by Roberta Tinkham

Published by Vantage Press, Inc.
516 West 34th Street, New York, New York 10001

Manufactured in the United States of America
ISBN: 0-533-11167-6

Library of Congress Catalog Card No.: 94-90264

0 9 8 7 6 5 4 3 2 1

To Mary Brown Tinkham

Cliff

When I think of you,
I get very glad your
life crossed mine
I am very thankfull
for every thing you
have done to help me.
I thank god everytime
I think of you.

Contents

Discovery and Other Poems

Love Bubble

Love is like a big bubble,
Floating on the air,
Drifting ever onward,
But not knowing where.
Just sailing through the vastness,
An unearthly thing,
With no thought of the future,
Or what it might bring.

Just a bright, shiny bubble,
Winds of chance may blow it high,
Perhaps it will drift out of sight,
Into the far-flung sky.
A glistening rainbow bubble,
It causes hearts to ache,
When pale hands reach to grasp it,
It's surely bound to break!

And then, my dears, what's left?
Nothing! The lovelorn turn to cry,
And raising their pale, forlorn hands,
They gaze into the sky!
What can they seek up there, you ask?
My dears, I'd say 'twas trouble,
Unsatisfied, they're reaching for
Another shiny bubble!

On the Dunes

One summer afternoon I strolled
Along a sandy shore . . .
Watched a seagull's lonely flight
And heard the breakers' roar.

Felt the cool, clean wind that sang
A gypsy song that day . . .
I lingered by the water's edge,
And wished that I could stay.

Unforgivable

Harold is a model boy,
He doesn't drink or smoke;
He very, very seldom swears
Or tells a shady joke.

He's sociable and dresses well,
At dancing is supreme;
He's a football hero too,
And captain of the team.

Harold is a handsome lad,
As handsome as they come,
But, oh, my dear, when he makes love . . .
He's always chewing gum!

Discovery

I've always loved to listen
To pattering drops of rain,
I've thrilled to hear a robin,
Warbling in the lane.

Night wind has held me breathless,
As it whispered to the trees,
But, now I've heard your voice, my dear,
A sweeter sound than these.

Somebody Wonders

I wonder why you are so shy,
And never look at me;
Are you in dread to raise your head,
For fear of what you'll see?

Each time we meet, upon the street,
You hurriedly go by,
Averted face, and quickened pace,
I pause and wonder why.

To talk with you, and walk with you,
I really wouldn't dare,
For all the while, you never smile,
And straight ahead you stare.

Perhaps you are a bashful soul,
Perhaps you're being proud,
Or . . . can it be, if you looked at me,
You'd have to laugh out loud?

Explanatory Note

There's music surging in my heart!
There's rapture sweet and new!
There's loveliness in common things,
Whenever I'm with you!

No doubt, you're very charming, but . . .
The explanation's clear;
It's just that I'm in love with Love,
And you're so handy, dear.

Reminder

Come, search in all those hidden nooks,
And bring out your forgotten books.
You'll soon be on your way,
Now September's in the air,
You must hurry and prepare,
For an eventful day.

Get your pencil and your pen,
Buy a notebook once again,
The school door's swinging wide . . .
Don't be gloomy—don't be sad,
It won't be so very bad . . .
Once you get inside!

Recollection

As I grow old, my memories
Of you will fade away;
I shall forget your tender glance,
Your laughter young and gay.
I shall forget the whispered words
Of romance that we knew;
And all the love songs that we sang
Shall be forgotten too.
Just something small, I shall recall,
Of all you've ever been;
How could I possibly forget
That dimple in your chin?

In Praise of Men
(It's the man who pays)

Straight from a shoulder not-so-cold,
Right from a heart that's spacious,
I'd like to tell you gentlemen,
(Now that I'm feeling gracious)
That I could call you lots of names,
But they would all be lies,
And anyhow, you'd guess the truth
If you looked in my eyes. . . .
And so I say you're wonderful,
You're Heaven's prize creation,
And every time you saunter by
I gaze in admiration. . . .
Because I think you're pretty nice,
In fact, I think you're swell,
Step right up, I'll pin a rose
On every coat lapel,
To tell you that you're charming,
Ah, yes, and mighty fine,
Especially when you come around,
And take me out to dine.

Winter-Proof

Sharp winds of January blow,
Against my window pane,
But if they try to chill my heart,
They'll blow and blow in vain.
For being modern in its love,
It's insulated through. . . .
With little dreams all snug and warm,
And cozy thoughts of you.

Monday Evening

Homeward bound at 5:15 . . .
My daily task is through,
My heart is filled with sweet content,
I'm tired, but happy too. . . .
Tonight there is no place to go
And not a thing to do,
Oh, happy thought, I'll sit and dream
A thousand dreams of you!

My Country Boy

Swinging on the garden gate,
Wind blowing through his hair,
I see a brown-skinned country boy,
Who's waiting for me there.

He dare not come up to the house,
But the gate he calls,
My bashful, barefoot Romeo,
In faded overalls!

He grins as I come down the path,
His brown eyes fairly glow,
I'm dressed in white, his heart's delight!
He's often told me so!

Arm in arm, we stroll along,
The lonely moonlit vale,
From yonder apple orchard,
We hear a nightingale.

How I enjoy our nightly stroll,
Beneath the starlit skies,
For there's a light that hints of Love,
Within those dark, brown eyes!

Here, peace and quiet reign supreme,
No bustling city noise,
No streetcar din, nor factory smoke,
No rowdy city boys!

And so I love the countryside,
The woodland bird's sweet call—
And, oh—my brown-skinned country boy!
I love you best of all!!!

A Note to NASA

Soar some more for lunar lore;
Explore there as you will. . . .
The moonlight in my garden
Entrances me still!
Bring back a sack of moondust;
It comes as no surprise. . . .
For many a year, I've sat right here
With stardust in my eyes!

Red Sun

The afternoon draws to a close,
Now the day's near done,
And hanging low in the winter sky,
Is the red December sun.

A massive disk of crimson,
That faraway faintly glows,
And tints the overhanging clouds,
A rich and dim old rose.

It brings a restful solitude,
As slowly it departs,
While peacefulness and calm have come,
To melancholy hearts.

And all the weary souls gaze far
Into the ruddy west,
The old-rose clouds have lost their hue,
The sun sinks to its rest.

My dear, that glowing scarlet ball,
Has sunk beyond my view,
I hope the dim red winter sun,
Brought peacefulness to you.

The Good Companion

Ellen isn't beautiful,
She's just an average-looking girl,
With ordinary hair and eyes . . .
Yet all the boys pursue her,
Via telephone and personal calls,
She's ever in demand.
You wonder why? Then listen,
She's got what it takes. . . .
A pair of willing ears,
And a great sense of humor,
(You know . . .
She laughs at all their jokes.)

Midsummer Afternoon

Sun streaming through the windows,
Outside the soft warm breeze,
Blowing from the southlands,
Rustling through the trees.

The suburbs' streets are quiet,
Scarce a noise can be heard,
Save now and then the sleepy chirp,
Of a lazy summer bird.

The big white clouds roll gently,
Along their sea of blue,
The daises in the prairie,
Blaze forth their golden hue.

How gently beautiful they are—
These things of which I croon,
The trees, the skies, the golden flowers,
Midsummer afternoon!

Dear Neighbor

Dear neighbor, won't you smile at me,
As I pass by your way . . .
And wish me a good morning,
It's such a pleasant day.

And if you need some groceries,
From the village store,
I'll stop and get your order,
As I go by your door.

*   *   *

"Your garden is so lovely,
You're quite a flower-grower."
(But for goodness' sake, do you intend,
To bring back my lawn mower?)

"Ah, yes, your baby's awfully cute,
A darling, and a dear!"
(The darn kid wakes me up at night,
When those odd yells I hear.)

"I want to thank you, neighbor,
For sending in that cake."
(Please don't send in another one,
It was tougher than flank steak.)

"Well, neighbor, I'll be on my way,
I've got a lot to do."
(Ye Gods, I can't stand here all day,
And chew the rag with you.)

18

Spring Song

The birds have come back from the South,
They're singing songs of cheer,
The leaves and blossoms are in bud,
Sprightly Spring is here!

A jolly sun and bright blue skies,
Brighten up the day,
And in the fields, the frisky lambs—
Are leaping in their play!

And in the village streets, I see
The little girls and boys,
Who laugh and play, the live-long day,
Content with youthful joys.

While lying on the hilltop,
Watching the clouds above,
A lazy youth is dreaming,
Of romance and of love!

"Hey, you, the sprightly season's here!
So laugh, and shout, and sing!
Get up and play, enjoy while you may—
The glorious days of Spring!"

Streetcar Oddity
(January 1936)

Transportation, not much speed,
But seven cents is all you need,
Pay your fare and step inside,
See everyday folks on an everyday ride.
On straw seats and in the aisle,
They come in every size and style,
Black and white, short and tall,
Look about, you'll see them all.

A mailman hanging on a strap,
A baby in its mother's lap,
The darky with the sad-eyed stare,
The salesman with the well-combed hair.
An office girl with weary eye,
The shipping clerk without a tie,
A laborer: PWA,
The schoolgirl in a red beret.

All these types and many more,
But what's that standing by the door?
And how do you suppose he got in here?
He's actually wearing spats, my dear!
I dare say it's a bit of a slam,
For a gent like him to ride the tram,
Bah Jove! Now what do you make of that . . .
With the monocle and the derby hat!???

Summer Girl

We all know a summer girl,
Light and gay and in a whirl,
Off for tennis or a swim,
Full of youthful pep and vim.

Eager for all active sports,
Cycling in a shirt and shorts,
Taking hikes o'er hills and vales,
And horseback rides on forest trails.

*   *   *

Then to the country club she'll go,
To dance beneath the lantern glow,
In pale green organdy and lace,
With glowing eyes and sun-kissed face.

Oh, many a bachelor heart grows weak,
And many a stag line's morals creak. . . .
As she would give each one a chance,
To lead her through a lilting dance.

Her best beau, knowing well her charm,
Firmly leads her by the arm,
Out to the swing, where he will croon
A love song 'neath the summer moon!

Dear Thief

This valentine I send to you,
Is minus the red heart,
For I am sadly missing
That most important part.

You are the guilty person,
Whom I have traced it to,
You disappeared quite suddenly,
And took my heart with you.

Come back, you charming robber;
Do you call this fair play?
You stole my one and only heart,
And then you ran away!

My Christmas Tree

With scintillating finery,
I've decked my lovely Christmas tree,
Big shiny balls of scarlet hue,
Bright ornaments of orange and blue,
Between the boughs of evergreen,
The tinsel sends its golden sheen,
And from the branches up on high,
Hang figures that appear to fly,
Canary birds bounce on their springs,
And angels spread their silver wings.

Each light sends forth a glittering beam,
A fascinating, tinted gleam,
That casts its individual glow,
On silvery icicles below.
Ah! Gazing at my lovely tree
Through half-closed lids, I seem to see
A rainbow-colored shimmering sheen.
With interlacing evergreen!

My gaze sweeps upward to the height,
Where gleams a Christmas star so white,
And sounding softly on my ear,
The tuneful Christmas bells I hear,
The little chimes which I have strung,
And on the lower branches hung,
They tinkle now as they entwine,
This lovely Christmas tree of mine.

A Ride on the Moon

The night is dark and peaceful,
A gypsy song I croon . . .
A dreaming, wondering melody,
To you, September Moon!

You sail so slow and silently,
Along your deep blue sea,
So all alone, yet steady,
So unconcerned and free.

I'd like to sit between your horns,
And sail away to Mars,
And I'd drop in and say hello
To all the little stars.

I'd sail behind the hazy clouds,
Those webs of silken gray,
The wind so strong would take me along,
To the mystic Milky Way.

And after my ride through the dark, night skies,
With the hour growing late,
I'd borrow a golden moonbeam, and
Ride home to my garden gate.

September Moon, so mellow,
I sing my gypsy song,
Hoping some dark and peaceful night,
You'll beckon and take me along!

Lazy Days
(A plea to thin, overworked humans)

Once more I greet a sunny sky,
And see the swallows soar on high,
The friendly sun is at its height,
And gleams a brilliant, dazzling white,
While all along my walk, the trees
Sigh and murmur in the breeze,
For these are lazy summer hours,
When Nature brings forth all her powers,
And wants us to enjoy her sights,
The golden days, the starlit nights,
And wants us to know Recreation—
All through the long summer vacation,
So, classmates, up and follow me!
Let's see how lazy we can be!

Let's doze upon a sunlit beach,
With ice-cream cones within our reach,
And when we choose, we'll sail away,
To Sleepy Hollow, o'er the bay,
Where we can rest beneath the shade,
And sip at ice-cold lemonade.
Ah, comrades! To our boat once more,
We'll sail to yonder breezy shore,
For there the grass is fresh and green,
And we can rest and be serene,
While gazing out upon the lake,
We'll dine on wieners, pop, and cake!
And when we all begin to doze,
We'll lie right down in our old clothes,
And then we'll start in counting sheep,
Until we drop off for a sleep!

Ah, friends! You may know better ways,
To spend your lazy summer days,
But come!! Try my way for a while—
Perhaps you'll even learn to smile—
My poor thin friends! Don't be high-hat.
Come, do this, and you'll all get fat!!!

Likable

I like you, I like your smile,
I like your eyes of brown,
I like your hair, so very fair,
I even like your frown.

I like the way you whistle,
As you stride along the walk,
I like the way you wear your clothes,
And like the way you talk.

Why, I like any song you sing,
Because it's sung by you,
In fact, I've found there's something nice,
In everything you do.

You really are quite likable,
And after all, you see,
I like you, my dear, because . . .
I know that you like me!

A Twilight in October

*(Inspired by a song and a boy
and a dusky twilight)*

October's dusky twilight,
Is closing 'round the town,
And lazily the tinted leaves,
Come softly floating down.

A mourning dove coos sadly,
Its slow sweet song persists,
Throughout the fading twilight,
Coming softly through the mists.

Far on the western skyline,
Glows the last, dim purple light,
Then gradually it wearies, and—
Dusk deepens into night!

I sit here by my window,
Dreaming and thinking—oh, hark!
Along the walk comes Young Romance,
And he's whistling in the dark!

Optimism of Mr. O. Sumdoe

Spring is here! Spring is here!
Skies are no longer dull and drear,
A smiling sun shines from above,
Oh, 'tis the season for sweet love . . .
(That's what the poets say).
But here I am in a sorry state,
My bill collectors just won't wait,
In all my dreams their faces leer,
I think I need a stein of beer,
To drive my blues away.

Oh, Spring is here! Spring is here!
Now that I've had my stein of beer,
I really hear the robins sing,
And take new joy in everything,
In fact, I'm very gay!
I just don't worry about those bills,
To think of them gives me the chills,
If they're not paid, I know darn well,
I'll spend the summer in a nice cool cell,
Oh, Spring is here! Hey! Hey!

I Missed My Train Again!

I sit in the dumpy station,
Outside is the dripping rain,
I'm cussin' 'cause I scarcely missed,
That doggone northbound train!

The 7:25 it was,
But now I have to wait,
And sit in this filthy station,
Till ten minutes after eight!

Ye Gods, why am I such a fool?
As to waste the time away?
And go on ever missing trains,
In the same old droopy way?

Oh, why am I so foolish?
A second or so too late—
When I know darn well,
I'll have to run like hell,
'Cause the doggone train won't wait!!!

Vacation Thoughts

Happy times and lazy hours,
Of quite a long duration,
All students now enjoy them, for
'Tis long summer vacation!

Some will journey eastward,
The sea is at its best;
Others long for mountains,
And travel to the west.

The ones who aren't so prosperous,
But full of pep and vim,
Abide in lakeside cottages,
And play and dance and swim.

Ah, there they go, the happy kids,
Hurrying to the station—
The train pulls in, they climb aboard,
They're off on their vacation!

Youth, Beware of Dreamers

Look ahead to the future,
Your life has just begun,
Childhood days have faded
Oh, Youth, you're twenty-one!

You're at the First Beginning,
Take any road you choose,
March on ahead, and don't look back,
And Youth, you cannot lose.

Avoid the little by-ways,
They are not what they seem,
And though they beckon prettily,
They lead but to a dream.

The by-ways are for dreamers,
Contented with a song,
But for the more ambitious,
The way is hard and long.

So, Youth, with your ambition,
Stick to the widest way,
The road is rough, the dust is thick,
But you won't go astray.

And if you meet a dreamer,
With stardust in his eyes,
Don't let him coax you from your way,
No matter how he tries.

No doubt upon his lazy brow,
The sunlight will be gleaming,
But, Youth, beware, those starry eyes
Just got that way from dreaming.

The song he sings is glorious,
I love it, I confess—
But, Youth, you're only twenty-one,
And you must have Success!

Tea Time in March

The sun is hidden by the clouds,
And night will come on soon;
The streets are drab and dreary,
On this chill March afternoon.

The leafless trees seem lonely,
The skies are cold and gray,
The last streak of light far in the west,
Is slowly fading away.
A homeless dog goes wandering by,
It's food he's looking for,
A mournful wind comes out of the north,
And rattles my cottage door.

The whole town seems so desolate,
So bleak and dull to me,
Now I see it's five o'clock
It's time to take my tea!

My Books

All those friendly storybooks . . .
Standing on the shelf . . .
Compose for me a lovely world,
In which I lose myself.

A thrilling mystery story,
A romance of the West . . .
Tales of faraway places,
Where all ships come to rest!

All these provide refreshment,
For my imagination . . .
And with a book I drift away
For rest and consolation.

I settle down into the depths
Of my big easy chair . . .
Oh, let the whole world pass me by,
I'm sure I will not care.

Let time roll on, let twilight fall,
And let my tea get cold . . .
Do you believe that I could leave
A story left untold?

I'll sit and burn the midnight oil,
While o'er my book I bend . . .
Lost within the tale it tells,
Until the very end!

First Day at the Fair

Good-bye, petty worries,
And good-bye, stupid care;
I'm out to have a splendid time,
I'm going to the Fair!

I'm taking all my money,
I'll spend it all, I know,
But I am very eager
To see this wondrous show.

I'll walk, and walk, and walk some more,
Along a magic way,
On and on, I must see all
In this one happy day!
My feet will hurt, my eyes be tired,
But it's my big ambition,
To feel I didn't get cheated on
That fifty-cent admission!

And when I'm home again, I'll flop
Into the nearest chair,
Kick off my shoes, and heave a sigh,
And say, "I've seen the Fair!"

Linda

The Gods of Beauty are not fair,
Here's one who got more than her share
Of Loveliness; the easy grace,
The queenly head and classic face . . .
Upon her did these Gods bestow
Two wondrous eyes that sometimes glow
With warm, brown tenderness, and sometimes flare
To anger in a cold brown stare . . .

Then, too, she has a lovely nose,
Lips like the petals of a rose,
A charming chin that knows just when
It should curve in, then out again,
A smooth young brow unmarked by care,
Above it all, her tawny hair,
Oh, this indeed is beauty rare!

But are her charms an outside scheme . . .
The artist's joy, the poet's dream?
Ah, no, that loveliness must dwell,
Somewhere within her heart as well,
To hold you in its magic spell . . .
And win your high esteem.

Expectation

From my hammock on the porch,
I see the twilight fall;
Feel a breath of evening wind,
And hear the last bird call.

Oh, magic hour of sweet suspense . . .
As I sit waiting for
That soft and quick, familiar sound,
Your footstep at my door.

Fair Warning

Our future has me worried,
I wonder if you'll mind,
Being wed to one who is
Artistically inclined.

I shall always have for you,
A love both sweet and strong,
And you shall oft be told of it,
In poetry and song.

For with my concertina,
I can give you a love tune;
And I can write a verse for you,
About the magic moon.

Oh, I can always whisper
Sweet nothings in your ear;
But at meal times, . . . please . . . oh, please,
Be patient with me, dear!!

Seeking Idealism

A strange sweet voice reechoes
When evening shadows fall,
And faithfully I follow,
That low persuasive call.

Across the windy prairie,
Under twilight's misty sky,
I venture, ever onward,
In search of that faint cry.

Oh, youthful eyes, gaze forward,
And stray not from the track;
Seek eagerly for that ahead,
And do not dare look back!

And if the cry grows dimmer,
And deep black night is near,
Look upward, ever upward,
Young hearts should feel no fear.

Now, gleaming in the darkness,
It doesn't look so far,
Gaze upward, and you'll find it,
Beyond the evening star!

Gloom and Joy of Winter

'Tis a gray day, a cold day,
The chill winds of winter blow,
The trees are swaying back and forth,
And earthward falls the snow.

The birds have all flown southward,
The trees are cold and bare,
Autumn months have passed away,
December's in the air!

Every flower has faded,
Seldom we see the sun,
But don't be sad and gloomy,
Winter is loads of fun!

Just think of all the downy snow,
The joy that sleigh rides bring,
And Hail!—To Old Man Winter!
The season's jolly King!

Christmas Bells

What is so softly, sweetly chiming?
Now on the breeze it swells,
Ah, time-worn songs that ne'er grow old,
Sung by the Christmas bells.

From out the belfry tower,
How joyfully they ring,
Glad music that is heralding,
The birthday of a King!

Ill-feeling and old prejudice,
From human souls departs,
Good will toward all their fellowmen,
Steals into human hearts.

Somehow, those happy Yuletide bells,
Make everyone believe,
That Christ is near, and sends us cheer,
On this, the Christmas Eve.

For even all the woebegones,
Hear what the music tells,
I hear their voices singing now,
In time with Christmas bells.

Awakening

Winter's past, the icy blast
Has vanished from my door,
So once again my heart is light,
I venture forth once more.

I feel again, the first spring rain,
So warmly, softly falling,
A robin perched upon the fence,
To his dear mate is calling.

My footsteps pass o'er velvet grass,
Fresh-watered by the rain,
I see the lovely pussy willows,
Growing by the lane.

Chill winter's gone, the lark's clear song
Rings out from hill and vale,
Sing on, sweet bird, and tell again
The springtime's cheerful tale.

Forgive Me

Forgive me, please forgive me,
I didn't mean to harden,
And make you think mean things of me,
Oh, dear, I beg your pardon!

When I said those horrid words,
I know I seemed uncouth—
But I was tired and angry,
In the foolishness of Youth!

I'm sorry, oh so sorry—
That I did fume and fret,
And act as though 'twas all your fault,
Oh, can't you please forget?

For Time will soon heal all the wounds,
My angry tongue did make—
So please say you forgive me, dear—
Or my poor heart will break!

Texas Man

He's a wild and woolly hombre,
From the Rancho X Bar X;
He's got a long and fancy name,
But we all call him Tex.

He's always full of bright remarks,
You've never heard 'em cuter,
And he likes to act on the business end,
Of a roaring, Colt six-shooter!

Every Saturday night, he starts a fight,
Down by the town saloon,
Then kisses the barkeep's daughter,
By the light of the full orange moon!

Now scrambling up the mountainside,
Now out upon the level—
He rides hell-bent-for-leather,
This dashing, reckless devil!

Ride on, ride on, young scalawag!
Make Whoopee while you can,
Live each day, and have your way,
You glorious Texas Man!

Query

You're practical and know so much
Of intricate machinery;
I wonder why you have no time,
To admire lovely scenery?

You've never really seen a star,
Nor felt the summer breeze,
You've never heard the wind's soft song,
Lingering in tall trees.

You've never watched a lone bird's flight
Across the sunset glow,
Nor felt the quiet mystery,
Of moonlight on the snow.

You've never heard the roaring surf,
Nor felt the flying spray,
Nor seen the twinkling harbor lights,
Across a foggy bay.

Why have you never climbed a hill,
A hill that's steep and high,
Just for the sake of that quick thrill,
Of being near the sky?

Why do I sit upon that hill,
To watch the Evening Star . . .
While you lie flat upon your back,
Beneath a motor car?

A Fairy Tale

Once upon a time—
  A fool there was whose heart contained
  A feeling sweet and tender,
  But he had such a stubborn pride,
  That he would not surrender.

  Ah . . . Love had dealt him a slight hurt,
  And though his heart did mourn,
  When e'er he met the lady fair,
  He gave her naught but scorn.

  And she was sad and much distressed,
  That he should treat her so,
  But soon she planned a woman's trick,
  To win back her lost beau.

  The next day as he strolled along,
  There came a great surprise,
  She stumbled into him, and raised
  Her lovely, pleading eyes.

  He cast aside his foolish pride,
  He raised his downcast head,
  He took her in his arms, and then
  Soon after they were wed.

  And then his days were filled with love,
  Sweet love, and tender laughter,
  And thus, he lived so happily
  Forever, ever after!

THE END

Starved Rock

Stairways cut in solid rock,
And sprinkled o'er with sand,
Wooded canyons, rugged depths,
That yawn on either hand.

The dark blue waters flowing past,
And how our hearts enjoy,
The splendid, far-flung vista
Of the River Illinois.

Historic plates that tell about
French settlers' exploration,
Of how the red men were besieged,
And died of slow starvation.

Wild roses grow in grassy plots,
Green moss climbs up cliff walls;
A dewy mist is in the air,
From sparkling silver falls.

Exaggerated scenery,
The canyon walls so steep,
Weird, forbidding, "Devil's Gulch,"
Romantic "Lovers' Leap."

But best of all majestic scenes,
Most wondrous of all sights,
The solemn, splendid, huge Starved Rock,
On lonely moonlit nights!

May Thoughts

I hear the wind a-rushing by,
It's calling me away,
To sunny fields and meadows,
On this blithesome day in May.

I want to run o'er rolling hills,
With green grass 'neath my feet,
I want to smell the clover,
So pure, and honey-sweet.

I want to feel upon my brow,
The cool, refreshing breeze,
And feel the graceful, prairie plants,
A-brushing past my knees.

I want to see some wind-blown clouds,
That sail along on high,
Like giant, downy powder-puffs,
That powder the blue sky.

But, alas! I must stick to my work,
And by my desk must stay . . .
Although I'm almost happy . . .
With these pleasant thoughts of May.

The Senior's Farewell

Oh, sing out my praises,
And give me three cheers . . .
I've finished the headwork
Of four long, hard years,
And I'm through here at old Empehi . . .
Now though I am proud,
And as glad as can be,
There's a queer little sumthin'
A wee part of me,
That is heaving a sad little sigh.

For it's farewell forever
To Empehi walls,
I've fought my last battle,
Through those crowded halls,
And now I am saying good-bye;
I've said my last say
In the class recitations,
I've balanced my last tray
Of Morgan Park rations
Remember the hash and the pie?

So-long to the gym,
With its athletic thrills,
The tricks on the ringers,
The games and the spills,
I ne'er knew I could be so spry . . .
Just one wish I make,
Now those school days are done,
If only the future,
Holds half as much fun,
As my days here in old Empehi!

Heat Wave

We swelter in a wave of heat,
Too hot to sleep, too hot to eat,
It's just like being down in Hades,
A-sipping ice-cold lemonades;
The water rolls from off our brows,
Exhausted, we just sit and drowse;
And wish that we were Eskimos,
Up where the Arctic Ocean flows;
For it would be so cool and nice,
To doze upon a cake of ice,
We'd even chaw on walrus meat,
To be there and escape this heat!

Cycle Fad

Everyone's on wheels these days,
Young and old alike;
You're quite passé, and out of date
If you don't ride a bike.

I see straight and bow-legs,
Of every shape and size,
Stiff legs unaccustomed
To sudden exercise.

All the cyclists puff along,
And pump for all they're worth,
The fat ones with the pleasant hope
Of lessening their girth.

Pedestrians on public walks
Aren't safe upon their feet;
The bike fans aren't responsible
For obstacles they meet.

A man can keep his self-respect,
If hit by an automobile,
But imagine his embarrassment
Being run down by a wheel!

They say it's just a passing fad,
For fat and thin alike;
Meanwhile, I haste to don my shorts
And go and rent a bike!

West Wind

Out of the west
A wind comes blowing,
Chasing the clouds on high,
Gaunt, ragged clouds
So swiftly going . . .
Racing across the sky.

Oh, what makes the wind
So wild and free . . .
With its uncontrollable joy,
Across the prairie,
It shrieks with glee . . .
Like an untamed gypsy boy.

And the fresh young voice
Of the wind is calling . . .
Calling me out to play,
To laugh aloud
With the boisterous breeze,
On this wide-awake wintry day!

While the wild, west wind
Goes merrily roaring,
Over the tops of the trees,
My carefree soul
Is upward soaring,
And racing along on the breeze.

It's an unrivaled joy
To be far from the crowd,
(Take it from one who knows)
To go sailing along
On top of a cloud,
When the untamed west wind blows!

Anniversary

O fragrant breeze that fills the air—
This magic night in June,
'Twas just a year ago I heard
A certain lovely tune . . .
You brought it to my very door,
A love song, sweet and low,
Can you recall that melody . . .
Of just a year ago?

Story with a Moral

"Save and have," Abe Lincoln said,
And so I brought a bank,
Put all my hard-earned dough inside,
And never smoked nor drank.

Of many a show and dainty bite,
I oft deprived myself,
My mon' went in that little can,
That stood upon the shelf.

"Some day I'll live in ease," thought I,
"And own a vast estate
Fine motor cars, and horses too,
And I won't speculate."

The years have passed, I've reached my goal,
My money pile's grown high,
But I'm not having any fun,
And here's the reason why.

Rich foods or sweets I must not have,
Nor strenuous exercise,
I must not even read a book,
For it will harm my eyes.

I must not take a walk at night,
For fear of catching cold,
With all my mon', I have no fun,
I'm eighty-eight years old!

At the Races

It's great to spend a day in May,
Gazing on new faces,
And mingling with the sporty crowd,
That goes to see the races!

Ah, what a thrill to yell, "They're off!"
And watch those ponies run,
Especially when your favorite bet,
Looks like the winning one!

To see them rounding that first turn,
Then down the stretch they speed,
A fat man's jumping up and down,
His horse is in the lead!

Such frenzy and excitement,
Oh, what an awful din!
As down the backstretch goes the field,
Which thoroughbred will win?

Great Scott! Look at that fat man,
He's simply going wild,
His face is red, his voice is hoarse,
He's acting like a child!

Down the old homestretch they pound,
Those ponies, sleek and fine,
The fat man's horse, a neck ahead,
Across the finish line!

Oh, what a race! Oh, what a race!
The fat man is much thinner!
He got a lot of exercise,
To see his horse the winner!

Passing of a Friend

Departed friend, the few brave years
We were together, you and I,
Were spent in laughter, not in tears,
Now is it fair for me to cry?

I hardly think it would fulfill
Your wishes, if I sobbed in woe;
When you, so pitifully ill . . .
Had yearned, no doubt, to go.

Contrast

Not long ago I looked at Life,
So wise and comprehending . . .
Always just a little bored,
And slightly condescending.

Now, I can only look at you,
And find it incidental . . .
That I should be so much in love,
And slightly sentimental.

March

Now fierce, young March comes blustering in,
Loud and stormy; raging through . . .
To chase the big, gray Winter out,
No timid month will do!

He roars and howls across the roofs;
But now and then comes swooping down,
To snatch a hat in windy glee . . .
While blowing Winter out of town!

Moonlight

Stealing o'er the mountains,
So silvery white,
A contrast to the shadows,
Of a deep, dark night.

Shimmering on the waters,
Set forth your ghostly hue,
A futuristic painting,
Of silver and blue.

Glowing on the gardens,
Of rainbow-tinted flowers,
A soft illumination—
Of fairy pools and bowers.

A soft, sweet song re-echoes,
Across the moonlit vale,
A haunting, tender melody,
The lonely nightingale!

June Night Reverie

Oh, how I love to rest my eyes,
On the mammoth orange moon,
That hangs so low in the starry skies,
On this glorious night of June.

The glowing stars are so restful,
After the long hard day,
They gleam, and beckon, and twinkle,
God's candles, lighting our way.

The sycamore's leaves are murmuring,
As the night breeze softly blows,
Carrying from out of the gardens
The scent of a full-blown rose.

And the sweetest stillness fills the earth,
Except for the crickets' cheeps,
Oh, where is my crooning Romeo?
Disgusting child!—He sleeps!

Fair Harbor

My heart was like a little ship
That sailed the stormy seas
Of Love, and found a Harbor Fair,
Where it could rest at ease.

You were that Harbor Fair, my love,
That peaceful port-of-call,
That offered shelter to my ship,
So weary and so small.

Long weeks my vessel lingered there,
Until one wind-blown day,
At break of dawn, I set my sails,
And softly stole away.

Far and wide, o'er running tide,
My little ship went sailing,
Seeking e'er a harbor fair,
And failing, always failing.

There's just one port for my small craft.
And there she shall return,
Cast anchor, and forever rest,
No more the waves to churn.

Your waiting hands shall tie her fast,
I'll be contented then;
In that same love, where I have found,
Fair Harbor, once again!

He Gave Me a Rose

He came all alone through the garden gate,
Wearing boyish and carefree clothes,
He came up the path, and onto the porch,
He smiled, and gave me a rose.

A beautiful soft and wind-blown rose,
He handed to me, and said,
"It looked so pretty, I picked it for you,"
Then he blushed, and bowed his head.

Thus I knew he was mine, to have and to hold,
And my heart sang with heavenly joy,
For at last I had won the true sweet love,
Of a bashful, country boy!

I Think Love Is Nertz!

Love is such a funny thing,
So joyful, yet it hurts,
Now in laughter, now in tears,
I think Love is nertz!

You bet, it's bound to hit you
And even though you've spunk,
Love knocks you out in no time,
I think Love's the bunk!

It puts you in a dizzy trance,
And makes the world seem hazy,
It numbs your brain, and grips your heart,
I think Love is crazy!

It makes poor men cry, "Darling,
I'll love you all my life!"
And when they wake up from the trance,
They find they've got a wife!

It makes poor gals shout, "Sweetheart,
I'll wash your dirty shirts."
Ah! Love is such a silly thing,
I think Love is nertz!

My Friend

It's great to have someone like you
To tell my joys and sorrows to . . .
Someone who greets me with a grin,
And sticks by me through thick and thin.
Who cheers me when I'm feeling sad.
And laughs with me when I am glad.
My friend, when you step in the room,
In streams the light; out stalks the gloom!
Cold, empty skies of dreary gray
Turn rosy when you come my way.
O Friend! Mere words will ne'er impart
The place you hold within my heart!
And as I live the long years through . . .
I often wonder what I'd do
Without a friend like you!

Dear Enemy

When you and I have a chance meeting,
You nod and give a sharp, curt greeting,
My own dear enemy,
And as I pass, I do the same,
But you're the real one to blame,
For lack of courtesy.

Because right from the very start,
I felt a pang deep in my heart,
A pang of sad regret,
For you were rude, and very vile,
In fact, you wouldn't even smile,
The first day that we met.

Now when you pass, you hang your head,
Why don't you lift it up instead . . .
And greet me with a grin?
Do you e'er think, dear enemy,
If you had acted nice to me . . .
What friends we might have been?

Disillusioned Debutante

I was a fool to fall in love,
And swear by all the stars above,
That I would e'er be true . . .
I was a fool when I believed
That I would never be deceived,
By such a love as you.

When I think back upon the time,
When I was wrapped in love sublime,
My pulse beats never flutter . . .
I know what once was part of me,
That breathless, headlong ecstasy,
Should now be in the gutter.

But I won't sob and mourn for you,
The way lost lovers usually do,
When soulful passion dies . . .
And when the gossips visit me,
I'll smile as I serve lemon tea,
And tell them little lies.

Absence

The warm night wind sings soft and low
   A mournful little tune,
The trees sigh broken little sighs,
   And mist is on the moon.

The tulips bend their lovely heads,
   And stars refuse to glow. . . .
The Night and I are sad, my dear,
   Because we miss you so.

High School Worry

Oh, he is only a 2.B.
And I am a 3.A.
Why did I ever fall for him?
How did I get this way?

Because he is so very young,
I feel like a cradle-snatcher,
And everyone will say that I'm—
A red-hot baby-catcher!

Oh, dear! He's so attractive!
I want him for my beau—
And even though he is so young,
I cannot let him go!

Perhaps if I pursue him,
He'll run home to his mother,
But even so I'll follow him,
He may have a big brother!!!

Engagement Ring

My heart is gay, this Autumn day,
Though rain may fall, and trees be bare,
Though no bird sings, I've joy enough,
In knowing that you care . . .
When I look down upon my hand,
And see the love-light there.

Through the Night

I stood alone beneath the wind-swept skies,
And dreamed the dream found only in your eyes,
While overhead the dark of night came creeping,
My eyes were dry, but my poor heart was weeping,
Then high above there gleamed the Evening Star,
I took new hope; it didn't look so far!

The eagerness that newborn courage grants
Was mine; and it led onward to Romance!
The misty path no longer did I fear : . .
My own suspense seemed like a ray of cheer,
Along a stardust trail my journey led,
The Evening Star still shining overhead.

Then suddenly the night began to pale,
And I had reached the ending of the trail,
Oh, so bewildering was the break of day . . .
My Evening Star was fading fast away . . .
I felt the winds of Dawn rush through my hair,
And then I turned to see you waiting there!

Thunderstorm

A big wind howls about the house,
And rattles every window pane,
Lightning flashes, thunder roars,
Then comes the swiftly beating rain.

And through it all, I have no fear
For I am cozy, dry and warm,
Nestled here beside you, dear,
So safe and sheltered from the storm.

Beyond My Courage

We walk along a crowded way,
And greet our friends in passing;
A rather common-looking person passes by . . .
I say, "Hello," and on we go.
Casually you question me,
"Who was that?" and I reply,
"Oh, that was Bill,
I've known him for years."
But that's a lie . . .
I never shall know him,
I cannot find his soul,
He is as deep and dark
As an undersea cavern . . .
And I've always been afraid
To swim in deep water.

In a Tavern

I saw you standing indolently there,
Against the bar, so poised and debonair
You were, I viewed you in alarm . . .
Right then and there, I felt your fatal charm.

My heart beat out a warning, for it knew
How quickly I could fall in love with you
Without half-trying—before one word was said.
(I blame it on the pose of your dark head.)

Whate'er it was, that sudden fascination,
That sweet and strange, that tender new sensation
Would not be quelled, but sent its silent plea.
You looked my way, and then you smiled at me.

Twilight in the Country
(Lake Shawano, Wisconsin)

Dreamy, dusky twilight,
With shadows on the hill,
Just before the stars come out,
And all the country's still.

The trees against the dark gray sky,
How black and lonesome they appear,
And there's the dusty country road,
Deserted, semidark, and drear.

While from the cottage windows,
The lamps so brightly glow,
And roundabout the countryside,
The shadows longer grow.

As I sit here on the door stoop,
I'm glad that I don't miss,
The gray and murky beauty,
Of a twilight such as this.

Drifting

(On Pine Lake, Indiana, August 8, 1933)

Upon the lake's blue waters,
So peacefully I float,
I feel so lazy drifting,
In my little open boat.

And as I slowly cruise along,
Contented and carefree,
I lift my gaze and look about,
And this is what I see—

The wide blue sweep of summer skies,
The gray gull's soaring flight,
The sunbeams dancing on the waves,
Ah,—what a wondrous sight!

The pine trees on the distant hills,
Their emerald beauty sway,
The water-lilies' virgin heads,
That float within the bay.

Then to the sounds of land and sea,
I lend a listening ear,
Small wonder that I drowse along,
For this is what I hear—

I hear the bubbling ripple,
Of the waves that rise and fall,
I hear the crickets' steady drone,
And then a cat-bird's call.

The lullaby of fluttering leaves,
Is wafted on the breeze,
And when I hear that restful song,
I know my heart's at ease.

And I am deeply grateful,
For all this I hear and see—
For Life is good, and Life is kind,
And Nature smiles at me.

Jigsaw Hearts

Oh, such a baffling problem,
You've broken them apart,
The many little pieces,
Of my jigsaw heart.

I had it all together once,
It took such time and care,
And when the whole thing was complete,
I breathed a little prayer.

A little prayer of thankfulness,
That I could start anew,
And give my whole heart to a love,
That would be sweet and true.

Alas, the day we met again
Beneath those turquoise skies,
I thought my heart was cured, and so
I looked into your eyes.

I'll ne'er forget your tender gaze,
Upon that day we met,
Those midnight eyes spoke of a love,
They could not quite forget.

But, quickly then, you went your way,
I heard a thump and then,
The pieces of my mended heart
All fell apart again!

This Year's Spring

This year's spring is lovelier
Than any I have ever known,
The blossoms are more fragrant now
Than any that have ever blown.

It seems to me the robin sings
More sweetly than did last year's bird,
Somewhere he's found a clearer note
Than any I have ever heard.

I know the secret of it all,
Just why the season is so fair . . .
For I have looked deep in your eyes,
And found the answer there.

The Visitor

In the middle of a dream,
When night was on the wane,
I 'woke to hear a gentle tap
Upon my window pane.

The rosy Dawn was dewy-fresh,
And fragrance filled the air,
A lovely maiden stood outside
With blossoms in her hair.

And as she turned and smiled at me,
I heard a bluebird sing,
I flung the casement open wide,
And in stepped the Spring!

Saturday Night on Main Street

Let's look into shop windows,
As we stroll up and down,
The Main Street of our village,
In drowsy Brainerd town.

You might think it a sleepy place,
And far from being bright,
But you should walk along this way,
On a good old Saturday night!

For then the place is seething,
With folks and motor cars,
And a vendor's on the corner,
Selling ice-cream bars!

Shop doors slam, and dogs do bark,
While children play and shout,
And drivers seek a place to park,
As cars pull in and out!

And then about twice an hour,
We see a mild sensation,
The railroad crossing bells ring out,
A train stops at the station!

When all the shoppers have gone home,
Main Street's again serene,
Just once a week we witness,
The exciting little scene!

And though we travel far and wide,
To places of renown,
We'll all come back for Saturday night,
In good old Brainerd town!

Memoirs of September

Those golden days of romance,
That I shall e'er remember,
When the leaves were falling,
In misty, sad September.

Dreamy skies brought tearful eyes,
Eyes that once knew joy,
Glowing, deep expressive eyes,
Which belonged to that dear boy.

Sunset trails, and windswept vales,
The song of the mountain dove,
All brought back sweet memories,
Of an idealistic love.

September night of soft moonlight,
You played a glamorous part,
Then suddenly faded, and left him with—
A broken, bleeding heart!

God's Country

Somewhere, not so far away,
There's a valley that I know;
Touched with colors of the sunset,
While the shadows longer grow.

What a lovely way to go . . .
Especially near close of day;
How simple there, to say a prayer;
Somewhere not so far away.

Halloween Night

The heavens are dark and somber,
With an orange moon on high,
'Tis the night of Halloween,
When witches ride the sky!

And the silhouette of a big black cat,
Is seen on the old fence rail,
And ghosts walk, and goblins stalk,
O'er every hill and vale.

While the night wind howls amongst the trees
And owls soar weirdly past,
And gliding along the ground are shadows,
That the swaying branches cast.

From a darkened cottage window,
Gleams a warm and friendly light;
It's our jolly, grinning pumpkin head,
That welcomes us home tonight!

But hark! Now we know it is midnight,
There's no mistaking that tune,
The big black cat on the old rail fence—
Is serenading the moon!

War on Poetry

It's not so bad to sing or dance,
To talk or paint or draw,
But writing poetry, my dears,
Should be against the law!

Everyone around me,
Is writing silly verse,
If I hear much more of it—
I'll be ready for the hearse!

Crazy words and jerky rhymes,
And full of simple stuff,
If someone shows me another poem,
I'm gonna get mighty tough!
So if I'm on the war path,
And looking quite malicious,
Some simple poem will be the cause,
Of my becoming vicious!

Poems, poems, poems,
They're all a lot of hooey!
Good gosh! I've written one myself—
Caramba! Double-Phooey!

February

Lonely skies so dull and drear,
Rough wind that whistles past my ear,
Cold and fierce unfriendly rain,
That beats against my window pane,
That's February!

Little sparrows of dull feather,
Seem to like this stormy weather,
And a fluffy chickadee,
Sitting in yon leafless tree,
Seems merry!

From my lips there comes a sigh,
As rain clouds gather in the sky,
Yet, somehow in my heart I feel—
A love that's deep, and strong, and real,
For this, our February!

Now in November

They told me Summer love would fade
As stars fade with the dawn.
They warned me not to cherish it,
For it soon would be gone.

How wrong they were who thought they knew!
My love goes on the same . . .
And every Autumn wind that blows
Is nourishing the flame.

At Christmastime

At Christmastime, do you recall
The breathless wonder of it all?
The crispy cold at break of dawn,
The small click of a lamp turned on,
Robes and slippers quickly donned?

O, what loveliness to see
The glow and glitter of the tree!
The treasures there for you and me!
At Christmastime, do you recall
The sweet enchantment of it all?

Sunset Reverie

O'er me comes a dreamy feeling,
As the sun sets in the west,
Spreading far and near its glory,
On the earth's sweet-flowing breast.
Never are they dark dreams,
That haunt and terrify,
Rather are they golden dreams,
To match the golden sky.

Dreams that carry me along,
On journeys of delight,
That shut out fear and evils,
Of a dark and dreadful night!

Oh, flaming disk of beauty,
Before I take my tea,
I thank you for the joyous dreams,
You bring to lonely me!

Blessed Event

It was so gracious of Him,
To give the best He had;
We hardly thought our hoping,
Would get us such a lad.

Through all the months of waiting,
We said a little prayer . . .
Humbly knowing we would take
Whatever He could spare.

He walked among the Cherubim,
And chose the sweetest one . . .
This dimpled, blue-eyed baby,
To be our little son!

Little Toy Men

Little toy men in the attic,
Remember your leader small?
He whose shout would order you about,
Suddenly has grown tall!

Little toy men in the attic,
Seems only yesterday . . .
Your Captain was here, with command so clear,
And now he's been called away.

Must Reality come so swiftly?
Little toy men, is it true?
Did he really look so tall today . . .
Wearing his Air-Force blue?

Season's Mission
(April 13, 1934)

This is a mission for each happy heart,
It is to seek out saddened fellowmen,
To comfort them with cool, refreshing hope,
And tell them that the springtime's come again.

The city streets are mournful with the tread,
Of melancholy footsteps, sad and slow,
There are so many now who need your smile,
So many burdened by the winter's woe.

They go about with downcast, lowered gaze,
Devoid of hope, and lost among the crowd,
Did you e'er guess it might be in your power,
To raise the head so pitifully bowed?

Ah, Happy Heart, your comrades need your joy,
So give a smile, and give a word of cheer,
If you can lift their tired gaze, perhaps
They'll look about and see that Spring is here.

Winter Sunset

Oh, dimly tinted winter sky,
Dull orange and apple-green,
Set off by billows of white snow—
A charming winter scene!

Far above the cold drear clouds,
Serenely sailing by,
A shepherd's flock of dull gray sheep
A-grazing in the sky!

Ah, see those gold and purple streaks,
That stretch for miles and miles,
And see those glowing amber groups
Of lovely coral isles.

I enjoy the gaudy sunsets,
Of summer, spring, and fall—
But the blending hues of a winter sky,
Are lovelier than them all!

The Old Bus
(Or, She Ain't What She Used to Be)

It's carried us for miles and miles,
Through country and through town,
No wonder that the poor old bus
Is slowly breaking down.

Although the body sags in back,
There's reason for decline,
The seats were made to carry five,
They've carried eight and nine.

It's taken us on summer trips,
And brought us back again,
It's also served as picnic bus,
To some cool forest glen.

It's been a movie-taxi,
And travelled to and fro
The Highland and our homestead,
So we could see the show.

Oh, I could ne'er name all the towns,
The old Nash has passed through,
But I remember annually,
It travelled to the Zoo.

Well, after all, now seven years,
Can change a point of view,
Our car no more has pep galore,
It's lost its figure too.

It's run its course, it's out of date,
For speed it does not care,
It has a hard time starting up,
Just like the old gray mare.

And when it slowly percolates,
Along the avenue,
The floor boards are not windproof,
A breeze comes blowing through.

The fresh-air jitney at its best,
Has given all it's got,
I really think it needs a rest,
Within a used-car lot.

We'll ne'er forget the old bus,
It's showed us so much fun,
But now we need a new car,
The old one's day is done.

Lovely Lake

*(Written in a summer cottage
by the shores of Lake Shawano,
Wisconsin)*

Lake Shawano, land o' dreams,
Far more romantic than it seems,
Where the cool waves lap the sun-kissed shore,
While over the island the seagulls soar.

From grassy hills comes the sighing breeze,
Laughing and whispering through the trees,
And the fleecy clouds up in the sky,
Are like shepherds' flocks that are passing by.

Oh, glistening waters and glorious sky,
It takes a better poet than I,
To describe your beauty and write a poem,
To inspire those whom we left back home!

Autumn

'Tis Autumn, spicy Autumn,
The fruitful season's here,
The time to gather in the crops,
And spread the harvest cheer.
To greet the hazy morning,
And watch the bright leaves fall,
To scan the skies overhead,
As you hear the wild duck's call.

To go a-hikin' in the woods,
And gather lots of nuts,
To see the comic turkey-bird,
As along the path he struts.

To build our heaping bonfires,
And while our wieners roast,
Have one of the bunch tell a yarn,
About a weird old Autumn ghost.

And watch the smoke curl upward,
From the depths of the burning leaves,
While a hoot-owl's wailing cry is heard.
From his nesting place, under the eaves.

Lone Tree at Dusk

Through December's cold gray twilight
Stretching leafless limbs on high
I can see a lone tree standing,
Etched against the evening sky.

As darkness falls, a snow bird calls
And I must hurry home,
And leave the solitary tree
Beneath night's velvet dome.

When I turn to look again,
While standing from afar,
I see the branches reaching out
To catch another star.

Next-Door Peonies

These flowers are a lovely sight,
Deep red, and pink, and snowy white,
A perfume scent they sweetly share
And spill their fragrance on the air.

Great fluffy blooms so bright and gay
They fairly take my breath away.
I've ne'er beheld such size and hue,
Oh, neighbor, may I have a few?

Umbrella Song

Welcome, April morning,
With sky so darkly gray,
It looks as though I shall enjoy,
A rainy walk today.
For I've a flowered parasol,
So colorful and gay,
The blossoms blooming overhead
Will chase the gloom away.

South Pole Returnee

Alan's back, and looking well,
And oh, what tales he has to tell!!
And slides to show . . . two hundred or more . . .
On scientific stuff galore;
On joy of comradery,
At Christmastime, they had a tree.
The fights, and feasting of the men;
Snow devils in his little den;
And waiting for a satellite,
In the long Antarctic night!!!

First Love

The postman walked up to my door
And brought what I'd been hoping for,
A lovely Valentine!

The red heart bore no signature,
Just rounded letters immature
That said, "Will you be mine?"

A missive from a bashful beau,
And how it set my heart aglow—
Though I was only nine!

Halloween

Loud and sharp the doorbell rings,
Nobody is there . . .
Just impish laughter echoing
Upon the Autumn air.
"Rat-a-tat-tat" little beans
Against the windows beat,
And then small goblins scurry
Along the darkened street.